**Macmillan/
Lif**

Animals That...
Fly, Crawl, Jump, & Swim

Frog jumping

AUTHORS

Mary Atwater
The University of Georgia
Prentice Baptiste
University of Houston
Lucy Daniel
Spindale Schools; Rutherfordton, NC
Jay Hackett
University of Northern Colorado

Richard Moyer
University of Michigan, Dearborn
Carol Takemoto
Los Angeles Unified School District
Nancy Wilson
Sacramento Unified School District

Butterfly

Macmillan/McGraw-Hill School Publishing Company
New York   Chicago   Columbus

Animals That...
Fly, Crawl, Jump, and Swim

Themes:
Patterns of Change / Scale and Structure

Lessons

Activities!

EXPLORE

TRY THIS

Crayfish

The pond

Animals With Jointed Legs

Where do you live? What might live under that big rock in the picture? What is on that leaf? These animals have jointed legs. They live and grow.

Minds On! Could you live in a pond? How is your home different from where a crayfish lives? ●

Let's look closer at a butterfly.

Activity!

Where Do Butterflies Come From?

Butterflies live in many places. You can see them on flowers. How do they grow and change?

What You Need

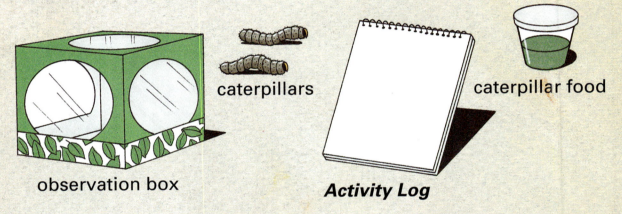

observation box

caterpillars

Activity Log

caterpillar food

What To Do

1. Put the box in a warm, dry place.

2. Place the caterpillars in the box. Draw a picture of them in your *Activity Log*.

3. Look in the box each day. When you see something new, draw it in your *Activity Log*.

4. Wait about three weeks. Draw a picture of the butterfly in your *Activity Log*.

Painted lady butterfly

What Happened?

1. What happened to the caterpillars?

2. Tell what happened when each butterfly came out of its case.

Many Insects Live in Our World

The butterfly you just watched in the Explore Activity is an **insect.** The tiniest animals you can see are insects. How can you tell if an animal is an insect? Let's look at some to find out.

All insects have six legs that can bend. Their bodies have three main parts.

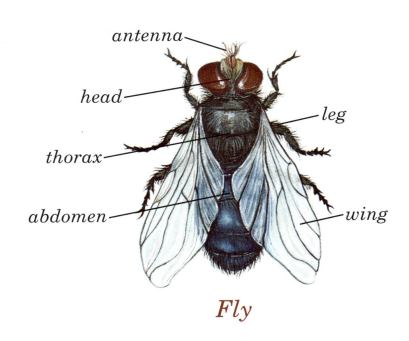

Fly

Insects breathe air and eat food. They use their antennae to sense their world.

Water strider

Insects move in different ways. Some have wings to fly, some crawl, some jump, and some skate across water.

Katydid

Many different kinds of insects live on Earth. They live in many different habitats. They are able to find air, food, water, and shelter in their habitats. This insect is a katydid. It lives in trees and bushes and eats the leaves. Do you see how much the katydid looks like a leaf?

 CAREERS **Insects Bigger Than Life**

Patrick Bremer is a sculptor. He makes giant insects.

Mr. Bremer studies an insect v-e-r-y carefully. Then he draws its picture. The drawings help him cut wood into shapes for the insect's body. Then he builds wings from thin wires.

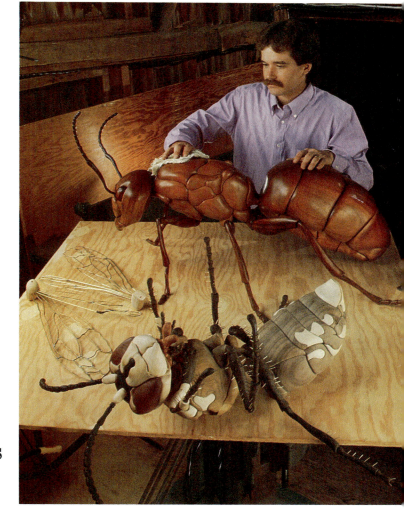

Butterflies Grow and Change

Insects, like other animals, grow and change. A butterfly goes through different stages in its life. Look at these pictures to see how a butterfly grows.

Monarch butterfly

1 A tiny egg is in a hidden place on a leaf.

2 A tiny caterpillar crawls out of the egg.

3 The caterpillar eats leaves and grows bigger.

4 One day the caterpillar sticks itself to a branch and hangs upside down.

5 The caterpillar's skin splits open. Under the old skin is a case called a chrysalis.

6 Time goes by and the case opens. Four wings unfold. The caterpillar has changed into a butterfly.

head

antenna

thorax

wing

abdomen

Butterfly

Soon the butterfly will lay some eggs. Can you tell what happens then?

Other Animals With Jointed Legs

Not all small animals are insects. Another kind of animal is a **spider.** A spider has eight legs. Many spiders spin webs in which they catch food.

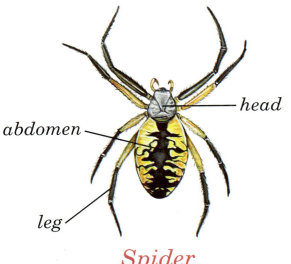

head

abdomen

leg

Spider

Spider in web

This is a trapdoor spider. It doesn't spin a web. It digs a hole in the ground. Then it grabs insects as they pass by and eats them.

Trapdoor spiders

You have looked at insects and spiders to see how they are alike and different. Now do the next activity to see if you can make models of them.

Cranefly

Spider

Activity!

Making Insect and Spider Models

What You Need

craft pipe cleaners

clay dough

newspapers

Think about the body parts that insects and spiders have. Use the clay dough and craft pipe cleaners to make models of each one. How are they alike? How are they different? Compare your models with others.

Thissssanimal is a centipede. See all its legs! Its body has many parts and each part has a pair of legs. Centipedes live in damp places. You can find them under stones or wood. They look for food at night.

Centipede

Millipedes look something like centipedes. They have more legs than centipedes, but they move more slowly. They also live under stones or wood. They eat plants or pieces of dead wood.

Millipede

How Are Animals With Jointed Legs Helpful and Harmful?

Many animals with jointed legs are helpful. Ladybugs eat other insects that harm some bushes and trees. Insects carry pollen from flower to flower.

Spider

Honeybee

Spiders eat many insects. Some people eat crayfish.

Many animals with jointed legs are harmful. Termites eat wood. They can cause poles or fence posts to fall down.

Termites

All animals are important to their habitats. If crayfish eat green plants and are also food for other animals in a pond, what would happen if all the crayfish were killed?

The pond

What Are Fish?

What animals live in a pond? If you stand very still, you might see a tiny perch or a bluegill swim by.

Minds On! Which is a better swimmer, a fish or a person? Why? •

14

Bluegills

Largemouth bass

Sticklebacks

F ish must
have water around them to
move, eat, and breathe. Do the next activity to
think more about fish.

Activity!

What Shapes Help Fish Swim?

Think about what fish look like. What shapes are they? Make a model to show the shape of a fish.

What You Need

string

tub of water

objects to test

Activity Log

What To Do

1. Tie a piece of string to one object.

2. Place the object near one end of the tub. Pull the object through the water.

3. Tie strings to other objects and pull them, too.

What Happened?

1. Which objects were easy to pull through the water?

2. Which objects were not as easy to pull?

How Can Fish Live in Water?

Think about the activity you just did on fish shapes. If you were a fish, would you want to be shaped like these fish? Do the next activity to make a fish model.

Activity!

Make a Model of a Fish

What You Need

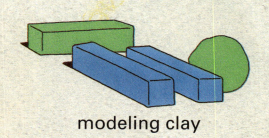

modeling clay

newspapers

Think about what a fish looks like. Remember the shapes of the objects that were easy to move through the water. Squeeze and mold your clay. Make it into a fish shape. Add the body parts you think a fish has. Share and talk about your model with a friend.

Most fish begin life as eggs. Usually fish lay their eggs and swim away. Look at these pictures to see how a fish hatches and grows.

1 Eggs are laid in a sticky bunch. The eggs grow into tiny fish.

2 Soon after the young fish hatch, they are able to swim. They eat tiny living things in the water.

3 Many little fish are eaten by larger fish. Some grow up and lay eggs. More young fish will hatch.

ook at the picture of the fish. How does its shape help it swim? Let's look at some body parts that help it live and move in water.

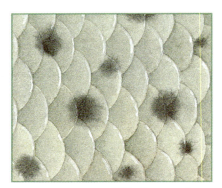
Fish scales

Most fish are covered with scales. Scales are hard and smooth. They protect the fish and help it swim.

Fish gills

Fish breathe through gills. The covers of the gills are behind the fish's eyes. Water comes in through its mouth and goes out through the gills. The gills take air out of the water.

Most fish swim fast. They swim by moving their wide tail fins back and forth. Fish also have fins on their backs, sides, and bellies.

Fish

Most fish have a skeleton made of bones inside their bodies. The bones give the fish its shape.

Fish skeleton

Minds On! Look at your fish model again. Do you want to change it? What would you add or take away? ●

Ways Fish Live Longer

Focus on Environment

Ladders for Fish?

Some fish go back to where they hatched to lay eggs. Salmon swim from the sea through rivers to lay eggs. People have built dams on some rivers. How can the salmon get around the dams? People have built ladders for the fish.

Fish jumping

Fish ladder, Bonneville Dam

Some fish have colors or body parts that let them live longer. The flounder is a fish that lives in the ocean. A young flounder has one eye on each side of its head. As the flounder grows, one eye slowly moves until both eyes are on the same side. Now the flounder can lie flat in the sand and hide.

Flounder

Minds On! What else helps the flounder hide? ●

What Are Amphibians?

What kind of animal do you see in the picture? See how far it jumps! Did you guess it was a frog? Frogs live in and near ponds. What do they get from this habitat?

Minds On! How does a frog swim? Tell how it is different from a fish. ●

L ook at
the frogs
in these pictures.
What can you tell about frogs?
Talk about the body parts you can see.
What do you think a frog's skin would feel like
if you touched it?

Activity!

How Does a Frog Move?

Think about the way a frog moves. You can make a model to show the way its legs work.

What You Need

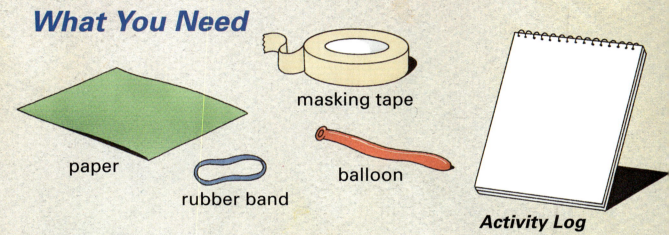

paper

rubber band

masking tape

balloon

Activity Log

What To Do

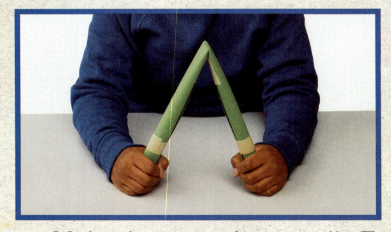

1. Make the paper into a roll. Tape the edges closed. Bend it in the middle.

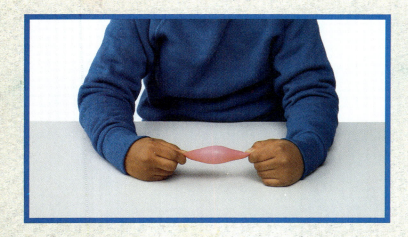

2. Blow up one long balloon slightly and tie it.

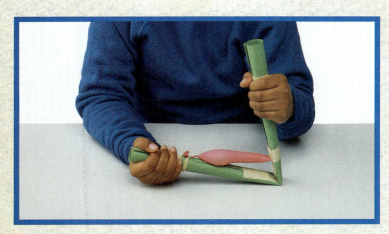

3. Fasten the balloon to the paper roll like this.

4. Pull the ends of the paper roll apart. What happens to the balloon? Draw a picture of it in your *Activity Log.*

What Happened?

1. How does this model work like a frog's leg?

2. What part of its body is the balloon like? How does this help a frog jump?

3. Can a fish move like a frog?

How Do Amphibians Live?

A frog is an **amphibian.** An amphibian begins life in the water. When it becomes an adult, it can live on land, too. Young frogs are called tadpoles. They look and act like fish when they hatch. They breathe through gills and have tails for swimming.

Frogs lay eggs in pond water. They do not stay to care for them. What do you see in the eggs? Do the activity to look at something like a frog's eggs.

1

Activity! Comparing Egg Models

What You Need

hard-boiled egg

spoon

tapioca

water

Put 3 spoonfuls of cooked tapioca in the water. Tapioca is like a frog's eggs. Feel the tapioca. Feel the chicken's egg. Tell how they are alike and different.

2 The tadpoles hatch. They eat tiny living things in the water. They grow larger.

3 The tadpole's back legs begin to grow. What does it look like now?

4 Now the tadpole has front legs, too. Lungs start to grow so the tadpole can breathe air.

5 This tadpole has become larger. What part still looks like a tadpole?

It may take up to two years for a tadpole to become an adult frog. Then it won't have a tail. It will always live near the pond, where it will catch insects and worms for food. Soon there will be new tadpoles.

Adult wood frog

Other Kinds of Amphibians

Tree toad

T oads and salamanders are amphibians, too. Toads usually have shorter legs than frogs and can't jump as far. What color is this toad? How do you think that helps it live in this habitat?

S alamanders usually have long tails. Many have brightly colored skin.

Northern red salamander

M ost amphibians live in wet areas. Some of them eat insects that can hurt people's food crops or carry disease. Be careful not to hurt amphibians you find!

What happens to animals that live in or near ponds when winter comes and the water freezes? Don't worry. The eggs of insects and spiders are safely hidden away. Many animals are alive below the ice and snow.

Pond in winter

Minds On! What do you think will happen when spring comes to the pond again? ●

Glossary/Index